PASSING THROUGH

Joseph P. Clancy

HEADLAND

First published in 2008
by
HEADLAND PUBLICATIONS
Tŷ Coch, Galltegfa,
Llanfwrog, Ruthin,
Denbighshire LL15 2AR

British Library Cataloguing in Publication Data.
A full CIP record for this book is available from the British Library
ISBN
978-1-902096-46-9

Printed in Great Britain by
L. Cocker Ltd.
Unit A9, Prospect Street, Liverpool L6 1AU

BY THE SAME AUTHOR

Poems
The Significance of Flesh: Poems 1950-1983
Here & There
Ordinary Time

Translations
The Odes and Epodes of Horace
Medieval Welsh Lyrics
The Earliest Welsh Poetry
Twentieth Century Welsh Poems
Living a Life: Selected Poems by Gwyn Thomas
The Plays of Saunders Lewis (4 vols.)
Bobi Jones: Selected Poems
The World of Kate Roberts
Saunders Lewis: Selected Poems
Where There's Love: Welsh Folk Poems of Love and Marriage
The Light in the Gloom: Poems and Prose by Alun Llywelyn-Williams
Medieval Welsh Poems c. 575-c. 1525

Non-Fiction
Pendragon: Arthur and His Britain
Other Words: Essays on Poetry and Translation

Short Stories (as P. G. Thomas)
The Retired Life

Novel (with Gertrude Clancy)
Death Is A Pilgrim: A Canterbury Tale

Contents

III. PORTRAITS

IV. A MATTER OF TIME

I. CALIFORNIA SUITE

for the clan that went west

HOMELAND

Americans who've moved to Wales,
    Native New Yorkers,
We find ourselves, on this first trip to California,
    In a foreign country.

San Francisco streets
    Are film-familiar, but the hills around
Turn brown for May.
    Come October, they'll be green again.

New York's bilingual these days, but history here
    Is half-Hispanic.
Today we passed a Mexican-style Methodist
    Church in main street.

As well, perhaps,
    Where papers feature daily earthquake forecasts,
To have one's cities
    Named after saints. Amid the Sans and Santas, though,

There's Sebastopol, Calistoga, Saint Helena.
    The last was christened
For a Russian princess. Calistoga
    Is a spoonerism:

The Saratoga,
    Its founder meant to say, of California.
As for Sebastopol,
    A local brawl reminded townsfolk of a siege

In the Crimean War. A splendid name, they thought it.
    Better than Pine Grove.
What's more American than self-invention
    And a fresh identity?

Some of our family
    Now make their home here. They take for granted
What surprises or amuses
    Our transient East Coast and expatriate eyes.

THE LISTENERS

Growing up in New York City in the thirties
We had two releases from our ordinary lives,
Apart from books and magazines. Movies

Were something we went to when we could afford it,
A family night out, but radio
Was a constant, familiar as the furniture

In our tenement living rooms.
Intimate, exotic. We tuned to
Voices from places that we had no wish

To realize. Driving through them now,
The cliffside homes, the level golden sands,
The palm-lined avenue

Neither thrill nor disappoint. What have they to do
With the names that charmed our childish ears?
Topanga. Santa Monica. Malibu.

CALIFORNIA DREAMING

The road unreels between the miles on miles
Of paradisal beach and porous cliff.

Carpe diem country. Houses
Impend above the highway, implants

In friable stone, flaunting their
Indifference to risk, refusal

To play it safe, readiness to pay the price
For views of the Pacific, disbelief

In gravity. Divers poised
On the highest board, breathing deep

Before the plunge, envisioning
The dissolution of the rock, the thrill

Of falling free until the film is
Paused, before the impact, to sustain them

In air above the pavement,
Rewinds them to resume

Their struts upon the hillside, overlooking
The sand, the ocean,

Rewards their levity,
Restores for them their frangible foundations.

FOG IN APPLEWOOD LANE

Miles inland, but the day begins
Within a cloud of sea breath. Going down the lane
To fetch the paper is an act of faith.

The apple trees on either side are Eden
Ghosts in the mist's high tide. Only the pavement
Grounding our feet assures us we exist.

But later, when we read the paper over breakfast,
The news will seem as evanescent as
The world we wakened to. Each morning here

Is meantime, in-between time,
A hush of genesis, beneficent cocoon,
Translucent shroud. Until the sun

Raises the curtain, frees us to resume
Familiar life, within the solid state
Our doubtful eyes are programmed to assume.

GEYSER

Privately owned. We pay the entrance fee,
In slacks and shorts and T-shirts file
Into the enclosure. Bare brown earth
Is hard beneath our sneakers and our sandals.

Behind, high walls of thick bamboo, and plumes
Of pampas grass. Beyond, the Palisades,
And the abandoned mines of Saint Helena.
We stroll about, prepare our cameras, wait,

Attend or not to the recorded voice
Explaining what we are about to witness.
Our eyes are on a patch of sodden ground,
The dimple at its centre. It performs

As promised. Puffs of steam, short spurts of water,
As though a javelin-thrower limbered up,
And then it hurls a jet some sixty feet above
Our gaping faces, sustains the spout for minutes

As cameras whir and click, before subsiding
Swiftly, falling back into its crack.
Some wisps of steam persist. We blink and stare
And wonder if we should applaud.

Once is not enough. For twenty minutes
We stroll once more and chat, we take
Each other's pictures, dwarfed by the bamboo,
We use the rest rooms, as the tape

Informs us yet again that barometric pressure,
The moon and tides, the earth's tectonic stresses
Determine the eruptions. Deep below our feet
Hot magma boils a river till hot water

Ascends again, on schedule. Satisfied,
We make for the exit, pause, and linger,
Attracted by a pen of Fainting Goats.
They stare back and refuse to faint for us.

GLOAMING

After a dayful of birdsong, woodpecker drill,
Swoop of swift and swallow, soar
Of hawk and turkey vulture,

Five humming-birds in the dusk
Come flitter-hovering above
The crimson bristles of a bottlebrush,

And in the west a skein of clouds
Feathers the evening sky.

MISSION

San Francisco Solano, Sonoma

Blood. A whitewashed chapel,
Hand-made, with straw and sun-baked clay,
And blood.

End of the trail. Twenty-first and last
Station on the *camino real*,
Way of the king, way of the cross,
That twisted northwards, serpentine,
Through a California Eden, christening
Its naked souls for God, its fertile
Soil for Spain.

The parish church is elsewhere now.
The State Park System
Maintains the buildings, barracks turned museum.
Within the chapel, crucifix and altar
Can still compel to prayer.

Have mercy, Lord,
On all whose bloodied feet and hands,
All whose bare brown flagellated backs
Have made this still a consecrated place,
And us, whose tourist curiosity
Has brought us here.

AMERICAN ADAM

Luther Burbank,
New England born and bred,
At twenty-six transplanted
Himself and his potato
To the deep soil of the Sonoma Valley,
The chosen spot of all this earth.

Self-taught pioneer,
Eden, for him, was not a finished product,
A leisure centre,
But a starting point, workplace, nursery
For Paradise.
Unnatural to leave
Nature untouched, untampered with.
Why else had he been graced
With green fingers?

God's surrogate,
His soiled hands blessed
Hybrids, and bade them fructify,
Fresh strains
Of peach and plum, quince and cherry,
Tomato, squash, asparagus,
Lily and daisy.

Innocent eugenicist,
Here in Santa Rosa
The breeds he taught to cross and flourish keep
His memory green.

REDWOODS

No birdsong. Insect hum, occasional
Rustles in the underbrush, our footsteps'
Scuffle through the duff define the silence.

We must look up to them. The austerity
Of the trunks. The aloofness of the branches.
Cathedral. Temple. Sacred grove. The awe

Is real. To name it is to smother
This otherness that draws us, up,
Up beyond the unseen crown, that drives us

Down among the unseen intertwining roots,
Into an unpeopled world, before
The mammals, before some dinosaurs

Took to the air. It stills the mind's
White noise, diminishes
Our centuries to insignificance.

Yet they are at our mercy. We have hauled them
Into our history, harvested
With choppers, sawyers, peelers,

Preserved this patch like others for
Our recreation. It abides
Our definition. Theme park, relic,

A shrine wherein to contemplate
The godhead beyond God, a place
To hike through or to picnic in,

Remains, reminder, woods we walk
In shadow, graced
When sunlight filters through the canopy.

AT BODEGA BAY

1. Most days, back home in Wales, when the weather's decent,
We stroll the prom, pause here and there to gaze

Out over Cardigan Bay. Some days the tides
Have left their relicts, and we pick our way

Through piles of sand and pebbles.
Ireland, unseen,

Is a breakwater, keeping the Atlantic off,
But now and then the ocean makes its mark.

2. Land ends abruptly here. A steep
Drop to a narrow patch of shingled beach
And rocks that bare black teeth at the Pacific.

It is, today, a tranquil ocean. Not a hint
Of the immensity beyond the bland
Verge of the horizon. Somewhere far

Out there, a century ago, men drew
A line, devised where day begins,
On the indifferent waters. Timeless, tameless,

Calmly, through this sunlit afternoon,
The waves below determine land's
Beginning, and its end.

3. Living beside a bay, or simply visiting,
Can put you in your place. After facing

The ebb and flow, envisaging the vast
Obliterating ocean,

We turn back to the daily round, defined, reminded
To ground ourselves in time.

TIME TO GO

Another sunshine day. The California oaks
Contort their limbs like Arthur Rackham prints
Against the blue, blue sky.

A single amaryllis flares beside the path
Down to the pool. Three tiny lizards
Sunbathe or skitter on the rocks.

Four hawks hang-glide above. A snail
Hunches its stolid way across the concrete.
The water lisps. We sit to read, or doze.

A few weeks here, a surfeit of fine weather,
And we are homesick for the fickle
Skies of Wales.

II. MUSEUM PIECES

for Dewi Stephen Jones

BALL

Encased in glass, out of reach, it makes
Our fingers itch
To touch, to close about its round
And heft it in our palms.

What was it for? What matter? Four
Millennia ago,
The maker saw within one lump of stone
A possibility,

And chipped and smoothed until he set it free,
A keepsake time
Has tossed to us, a toy to gratify
The transient mind and eye.

THE BUTTERFLY CONNECTION

Brown leaf on green. Easy to disregard
In this artificial rainforest,

Till it displays the facing pages
Of an illuminated manuscript.

Read me, it says. I am an open book
To those who know the language.

CELTIC CROSS

Standing tall before the gate,
It steers errant feet, hewn mirror,
Into a grave-strewn circle
Embracing the church's cross.

Its shaft is storied. The Fall,
The primal murder, Moses
Dowsing water from the rock,
Virgin and Child, the wise men
Adoring their infant Lord,
Thomas, one hand extended
To pierce Jesus' wounded side.

Steady compass, it directs
Eyes to its crowning glory,
Creation's radiant centre,
Christ enthroned on transverse beams,
Earth held within, God incarnate,
Eternity's perfect round.

Intransigent artifact,
Archaeologists' treasure,
Ancestral totem salvaged
From time's tumulus, it abides,
Tranquil, sure of its ground.
Stone tree, worn by wind and rain,
It bears witness to salvation.

CEZANNE'S MOUNTAIN

Time and again he turns to painting bathers.
Not from life. They keep him at a distance,
Bare faceless forms, unshapely flesh at ease,
At one with trees and bushes that encompass them.

And turns back to the mountain, brush a prism.
Out there, in here, a text to be deciphered,
The motif that has chosen him since boyhood,
Never and always the same.

It keeps him at a distance, slopes unpeopled,
An object realized from his sensations,
A presence, sure and solid as an apple,
As in the elevated host at Mass each Sunday.

Slowly, each brush-stroke an inquisition,
With dabs and splodges, slowly, permanence
Is netted in the transiency of paint,
And he begins to see the Promised Land.

DONOR

All eyes are on the Child, who plumply sits
    Enthroned upon
His stolid Mother's lap. Standing at his left,
Three placid saints in gaudy robes adore him.

The Child himself is looking to his right,
    And condescends
To smile upon the man who paid the painter,
Down on his knees, his thick palms pressed together,

His pudgy face alight with piety.
    Did his eyes
Stray from the Host, at times, for a Pharisaic
Glance at his image, reckoning the cost

Substantial payment for a seat in heaven?
    Mockery
Comes too readily. Commissioning
The picture was not merely vanity.

It is a prayer of sorts. A hope. A vision
    Of his salvation.
Whatever may have happened after death,
He purchased here an immortality.

THE EXHUMATION OF THE MASTODON

He is there, within his painting,
Charles Willson Peale,
Who served at Valley Forge, portrayed
Washington at Yorktown with his generals,
And persuaded Jefferson to back this excavation
Of a flooded field.

He stands, white-shirted, with his children,
On the rim of the pit,
Pointing to where a bare-chested workman at the bottom
Upholds an enormous bone.
All are dwarfed, father and sons, servants and masters,
By the machine,
Huge wheel, chain of buckets, pyramid of poles,
The man-made dinosaur delving into time,
Hauling antiquity from millennia of mud
Into new age, new nation.

In Peale's museum, back in Philadelphia,
His son will later dine triumphant,
Toasting Americans' pre-eminence, beneath
The mastodon's assembled skeleton, the indifferent canopy
Of ancient bones.

FIELD OF CORN

Here in Dublin, Ohio, between
Tracts of restaurants and office buildings,
This green field's stringent rows arrest
The casual eye.

White, dead white. Not headstones,
Gigantic ears of corn,
Fabricated ripe and shucked, implanted
Where once a farmer sowed.

Installation, suburban elegy,
Artificial crop unstirred
By wind and rain, awaiting
No harvest festival.

Black on white, two crows alight
Upon a six-foot concrete ear.
They fly away. I am a lilliputian scarecrow
Amid the alien corn.

FUNERAL SOCKS

No odder, surely, than an Egyptian pharaoh's
Papyrus sandals, robe with gold rosettes,
Chair of ebony and ivory,
Three couches and four chariots and seven oars.

She stitched her name, as was the custom, in the border.
Easy to imagine her, Ann Evans, in the long
Winter of a Welsh hill farm,
Knitting these foot cosies, calmly making ready for death.

But what are they doing here, neatly labelled,
Exhibited under glass with baskets, quilts, and love spoons?
Did someone rob Ann Evans'
Grave, like the tomb of Tutankhamun?

Were the chill feet stripped of them before her burial?
Did sophisticated kin refuse to put them on?
Or did Ann Evans, at the last,
Think it more fitting to go barefoot to the grave?

HARPIST

Far from the Cyclades,
Erect upon his marble chair,

His eyeless marble face
Alert, impassive,

His marble hands at ease
Upon his stringless instrument,

He has stayed poised
Millennia to pluck

A silent melody from empty air.

HOPPER'S LIGHT

Maybe I am not very human. What I wanted to do
was to paint sunlight on the side of a house.
Edward Hopper

The colour of silence. Neither curse
Nor blessing.
Unforgiving, unreproving,

It discloses solitudes. In city offices,
On country roads,
In hotels, on trains, in cafeterias.

It illustrates a lighthouse, a row of shops
Early Sunday morning,
Illuminates an empty seaside room.

It clarifies the fronts and sides of houses.
It discovers
A woman's naked acquiescent flesh.

Unhopeful, undespairing. This, it declares,
Is how it is,
And how it is for now must be enough.

JESSE

Stiffly he reclines, eyes shut,
A work of art, a relic,
A sideshow lit for us, the visitors.

Over centuries
The paint has faded, and the giant form,
Carved from a single trunk of oak,
Has been castrated. Nothing now
Springs from his loins
Where once prodigious boughs ascended
To Mary and the Child.

We stroll into the twilight of the nave
And pause before
The ordinary cross above the altar. Jesse's
Testament is potent still.
Through him the Word of God took root
In flesh, in time.

LOOKING AT REMBRANDT

We view it from behind, the easel looming
In the foreground of the painting. Larger than the artist.
Beardless, blank-faced, brush in hand,
He stands at a distance, eyes upon his canvas. He contemplates
Possibilities.

The canvas is a window. He shares his world.
Bridal couple. Mennonite preacher. Slaughtered ox.
His goddesses sport crumpled flesh; his Good Samaritan
Ignores a defecating dog.
Doctors anatomize. Old women read their Bibles.
A small girl stares amid the press of the militia.
He shares with us his wife, his son, his mistress.

He shares himself. The canvas is a mirror.
As burgher, beggar, painter, saint, philosopher,
He looks at us to share, unsparing,
His looking at himself. We look and know in him,
From youth to age, ourselves, no better
Than he knows himself.

LOOKING FOR VERMEER

The music is unheard, but gentle sunshine graces
A young girl standing bowed before a virginal
And her grave instructor.
A mirror, on the wall above the instrument,
Permits a glimpse of easel, canvas, stool.
The painter is not there.

He is here, perhaps, beyond a drawn-back curtain,
Fashionably dressed, slashed doublet, bright red shoes,
Brush poised, immortalizing
Perhaps a daughter posed as Clio, laurel-crowned.
But his back's to us. What of him, not seen in the tableau,
Who paints the painter?

The ordinary self that worries over money,
Attends a meeting of the St Luke's Guild,
Serves in the militia,
Is kept off-canvas. His many children's hurly-burly,
The daily life with mother-in-law and wife,
He sets aside.

They look at him, and sometimes smile, the women
Wearing red hat, pearl earring, writing a letter,
Being offered wine,
As now they smile at us, who see him purely
In the tidiness of a room, the stillness of a moment,
The serenity of light.

MADONNA

No beauty here. No timeless grace.
Incarnation
Of grief and resignation,

A worn-out peasant face
Stares vacantly
At vacant flesh. The God-sent son,

Loved, and never understood.
No expectation
Of salvation. No annunciation

Of resurrection. Only the mild
Uncomprehending
Look of a mother who's outlived her child.

MISERICORDS

God's house should be, these makers thought,
A home for man as well, in all
His homeliness. And so they wrought
A scene within each choir stall,

A guildsman in his finest coat,
An alewife with her jug, a scrivener,
A weary pedlar pulling off his boot,
A countryman and cat beside a fire.

There, as the spirit's voices soared
Beyond the spire, each bottom-rest
Mutely, upon its underside,
Rejoiced in the reality of flesh.

MUSEUM GOING

Part of our holidays. Something to do,
Somewhere to go on rainy days.
Our untrained eyes
Pass over masterpieces, linger

On singular scenes and faces.
Today, a special exhibition:
The attendant
Admits some twenty at a time.

The traffic's a distraction as we roam
From room to room. Each painting begs
For solitude,
Calls us to sit and contemplate

How line and colour have converted time
And all that matters to a moment's space.
We move through crowds
Of brilliant instants in an hour, then retreat

To give our eyes and feet relief
In the cafeteria. We treat ourselves
To an overpriced snack
Before we stop for postcards in the shop.

Out in the daily world again, we blink
And take our bearings. Enough if we retain
One glowing image
As thankfully we make for bus or train.

RELIC

A single turret fingering the sky,
Remains of wall ribs, and a blind arcade
Above the stone-leaved arch, the entry's vacant mouth.

We stroll the sunlit cross of turf and broken pavement,
A massive greenprint pocked with plaques to mark
The nave, the tombs, the transepts, and the chapels,

The choir, the sanctuary. The gable wall's
Paired towers transmit nothing to the air.
Its pointed window frames a drift of cloud.

We have seen abbey ruins. This is not the same.
It is as though we strayed amid
The crumbling bones of God.

Within the half-light of the small museum
A Celtic cross-slab, a sarcophagus,
A tombstone carved with skeleton and spear,

And the sundered time-worn head of Jesus Christ.
His lips are calmly sealed. His eyes
Gaze blind, expecting resurrection.

SCREENS

Each screen defines a space
Wider than high, a trap to capture
Time, and transcend it.

The year parades its seasons in four panels.
Snow, stars, and cherry blossoms.
Waves break across the folds in spring and autumn.

Through pairs of six-fold screens
A river swirls, volcano flares, sky blossoms
With a thousand cranes.

Nothing's human here
Except the hand that painted, eye that sees,
One with the scene,

One within the screen
With the display of sun and moon and autumn grasses,
The world that must be folded up and put away.

SHRINE

If there's to be a Second Coming, this
Is where it should begin. Here,
At the Museum of American Art in Washington, D.C.,
Where the Throne of the Third Heaven is a beacon
Jesus can home in on.

He sometimes called himself Saint James.
James Hampton, army veteran, janitor,
Born in South Carolina, raised a Baptist.
He heard the word of God. He set it down
In cryptic script, the visions and instructions,
Rented a garage, and spent his final years devising
A non-denominational
Temple for the millennium.

The central throne is flanked by matching pairs of objects:
Moses, the Old Testament, the Law;
Jesus, the New Testament, and Grace.
Adam and Eve are there, the Virgin, and the Pope.
There's a set of wall-plaques for the prophets,
An opposite set for the apostles.
FEAR NOT, it says above the throne.

He fashioned it from what he could afford or scavenge,
Materials no worse than bronze or marble
For manifesting reverence, and revealing
The light of God. Wooden furniture and cardboard,
Gold and silver foil, bright purple paper, light bulbs,
Straight pins, upholstery tacks, and glue.
Home-made apocalypse. A sacred fabrication.

It gleams now, glass-encased, awaiting
The fullness of time. A curiosity. Museum showpiece.
But if there is a Second Coming, here
Is where it will begin, and everywhere
There's handiwork the maker's prayers made holy.

VOYEUR

Degas' women are not nudes, they are women without their clothes.
Francoise Cochin

Again, again, again, the woman
Steps from the bath, stoops to dry
Her leg, her foot, her thigh,

Turned away from the old man's blearing eye,
As though he, famous and unknown, had not
Directed her to turn away, desiring

No display, only the natural composure
Of compact skin and sinew,
Wanting her faceless, feigning

A privacy, a purity,
An ordinary cleansing of the flesh.
She cannot wipe his gaze away, or ours.

III. PORTRAITS

BONE HUNTER

Edward Drinker Cope (1840-1897)

At seven, in a Philadelphia museum,
He sketches the skeleton of an ichthyosaur.
He looks into the empty sockets of its eyes
And knows his calling.

*

Beneath a sea of air that shimmers in the sun,
A wilderness of badlands:
Sandstone, siltstone, limestone, shales,
Once flood plain, swampy inlet, shallow ocean.

Deep in time's waters, illegible for millennia,
The bones await translation,
Erosion, resurrection, revelation,
A time that can decipher
The calendar of stone,
The grains within an aeon-glass, a change
Of time within the mind of man.

*

Land of midges and mosquitos.
At the touch of a pterodactyl finger
Extruding from the rock,
He is drawn deep within deep time
To read its legends.

Beside their campfire in the evening,
Quaker faith unshaken,

He reads from his Bible to the weary crew.

Before the mountains were settled,
Before the hills was I brought forth...
When he gave to the sea his decree,
When he appointed the foundations of the earth...

Wisdom. Sacred history.
It holds a deeper truth.

*

Back home in Haddonfield,
Husband, father, host,
He tells their guests at Sunday dinners
Of western hillsides chock-a-block with giant bones,
Of mountain men and bison,
How coyotes make the night
Musical, and skunks perfume it,
And how he entertained Crow chieftains
By taking out and putting back his teeth.

Frontiersman, pioneer,
In his Pine Street house become museum
As an ancient tortoise clumps about his study
He composes terse meticulous reports.
Collector from earth's crust of facts,
Adam of life's dream time,
He names his animals.

*

At Smoky Hill, Como Bluff, Bridger Basin,
Bone fever. Dinosaur rush. Fossil quarries.
Bones by the ton,
Minute and massive, bandaged, boxed,
Shipped east by rail
To be connected, classified, erected,
Dressed in conjecture,

To reconstruct in tranquil dry museum rooms
Their turbulent wetland's
Mindless world.

*

Feverish, at the Judith River,
He fondly writes to wife and daughter.
Can these bones live?
They come alive in dreams. Enormous beasts
That toss and trample him,
And in the small brain of a scuttling mammal
The possibility of love.

*

Distraction, the feud with Marsh,
Dogs snarling in a boneyard.
Disaster, investment in the silver mines,
Erosion of precious funds.
He must sell his collections, their house in Haddonfield,
Concede that Marsh has cornered
The market in old bones.

He rejoices in his daughter's marriage.
With saddle bags, blanket, canteen, and fish-net,
Straw hat, stout shoes and a good coat,
He sets out for the field again. Uncovers
Horses, camels, mastodons, and sloths,
Dines on venison and buffalo,
And listens to the mockingbirds.

*

What is man, that thou art mindful of him?
And the son of man, that thou visitest him?

In pain upon his cot,
Books and specimens an exoskeleton
In the museum room become his final home,
He contemplates the web
Of a colourless spider in the window corner
And slips into the silence.

PORTRAIT OF A SAINT

In paintings, always in the background,
Or behind the scenes. Always an old man,
As though virility might cast
Some doubt upon virginity.

I picture him as not quite middle-aged,
Good with his hands, perhaps a bit slow-witted,
An ordinary man to whom
Something extraordinary happened.

After the shock, the anger, the reproaches,
Whatever reassurance came in dreams,
He had to take her word. He made a home
And cherished her, he fostered Him,

Bewildered, often, by them both.
He didn't live to hear the preaching,
See the miracles. For him, the daily
Wonder of a wife, a child.

My father's patron saint, and mine.
I see him, sometimes, in my father's image.
Not that Dad was holy, or any handier than I am,
But in Joseph's place, I'm certain,

He would have acted much the same.
I am glad to bear his name.

PORTRAIT OF A DEAF AUTHOR

for Zachary Palisoc

We gaze, dumbfounded, blindly as his fingers
    Flicker. Illegible to us
His language. He watches as our mouths
Mime speech like fish in an aquarium,
        Shutting him out.

Behind the questing look and twisted lips,
    A foreign land. Yet, with mind's eye,
He attends the dance of words denied his ear,
And on a PC screen articulates a world
        For us to share.

THREE WOMEN IN OLD AGE

1. LOOKING OUT

For her, confined by age within
A third-floor flat,
This window is a television screen,
Her looking out
The looking at a world that she may enter
Only with her eyes.

Within the hillside's single tree
A blackbird warbles,
And finches flit from twig to twig.
Magpies and crows
Strut through hillslope grass. Gulls wheel and hover
Against a mackerel sky.

Cloudscape's a kaleidoscope, epitome
Of transient seasons.
She sees, some nights, a full moon float
Above the hillcrest,
And thinks herself looked in on, thankful for
These days of grace.

2. NONAGENARIAN

She must go out each day, no matter
What the weather. For a meal, to shop,
Go to church on Sunday, call on friends,
To have her hair done, visit the library,
Simply to be out.

Down the hill, teetering on spindly legs
In the middle of the road, avoiding
The unsteady pavement. She will not take
Her walking stick. It makes her look, she says,
Too old.

She confronts the town each morning
In floral prints. Her walk is brisk
Through younger stories. Shop windows mirror,
Within a time-scored face, the girl
She's always been.

3. TRANSIENT

From house to flat, from flat to single room,
Her body shrunken like her dwelling-place,

She awaits the last removal. It will not
Come soon. The stubborn flesh

Surrenders slowly, part by part.
Her mind's alert, though some days mist

Descends upon the valleys. She keeps,
For doctors, nurses, seldom visitors, a smile

Cheerful as her furnishings. Bright bedspread,
Gaily covered chair, TV with VTR,

Photographs of nieces, nephew, and their children,
Herself with friends now gone. There is no photo

Of the man she didn't marry. Her bedside book's
A Bible, but she calls herself, at eighty-nine,

A searcher still, certain only
That here we have no lasting home.

PORTRAIT OF A POET

for Bobi Jones

You're a foreign language. What should secular ears
Make of a bearded boy's
Sacred word-play? Your warp-drive verbs
Rocket objects out of irony's airless void
To a planet high in oxygen, a three-ring
Circus of a world where words
Prance and juggle on high wires
Without a net,
Fly at ease on syntactical trapezes, somersault
Through hoops of fire.

We flounder on your crests. We're blinded by your brine.
Yet your metres rise
Under us like dolphins, translate us
Breathless to a country where your spendthrift seeds
Have exploded into plains of grain, provision
For prodigals in every weather,
An Eden of love's groves and gardens,
And a rainforest maze
At whose tranquil heart stands a simple cross
Firmly rooted in earth.

PORTRAIT OF A PRIEST

for Father John Fitzgerald, O. Carm.

Every calling's a mystery, whether it summon
    In a blaze of tongues from the heart of a bush,
Or with still small voice once a whirlwind passes,
    Or by silent compulsion at a sudden crossroads
To take this path not that. Like it or not,
    A calling's not a career, no question of choice:
        One is chosen.

To serve the Word as priest, philosopher, and poet
    Is threefold a pastoral vocation.
You've rounded up stray adjectives and verbs
    And penned them in your intricate *corlannau*;
You've sheared the woolly mind; you've mastered
    The speech of diverse breeds, have even learned
        To baa in Basque.

Called to minister, with tenderness and wisdom
    These fifty years you've cherished wilful lambs.
Called to sacrifice, the sacrifice you've offered
    Is your daily self. May the Mystery who chose you
Accept, from this your motley flock, thanksgiving
    That in His providence, a means of grace for us,
        You were chosen.

BENEDICTA

(The German Jewish phenomenologist Edith Stein [1891-1942] became a Roman Catholic in 1922 and a Carmelite nun in 1933, taking the name Teresa Benedicta of the Cross. She was canonized as 'confessor and martyr' by Pope John Paul II in 1998.)

Arrested in Echt.
Transported to Westerbork.
Died in Auschwitz.

Leaving Carmel under guard,
The escape they'd sought to Switzerland denied,
Come, she said to her sister,
We are going for our people.

From the camp at Westerbork
She wrote to ask for woolen stockings,
Blankets, towels, and wash cloths,
A cross for Rosa, and a rosary.
She comforted the mothers.
She combed the children's hair.
So far, she wrote, I have been able
To pray gloriously.

The freight to Auschwitz switched at Breslau,
Her home town,
Where Jews were burned five hundred years before.
She stood,
Yellow star on dark brown habit,
Framed in the flesh-crammed stinking boxcar's
Open doorway.
We are riding to our death, she said.

*

Chosen.
It signified for her, as for her mother,
That she was born on Yom Kippur,
Day of Atonement.

I will let you find me, says the Lord.

Atheist in her teens,
Her only prayer, she said, was her search for truth.
Philosophy revealed
The possibility of God.
Nurse in an army hospital, she ministered
To the sufferings of the flesh.
She witnessed, in an ordinary woman's
Solitary prayer in a cathedral,
Conversation.
The night she read Teresa of Avila's story,
This is the truth, she said.

Empathy.
God as a loving Person to be loved,
Known
In the living body of the Jew on the cross.
She was christened
Into her people's history.

To her, fulfillment. To her observant mother,
Betrayal on betrayal.
In the darkness of faith, she said,
In deep peace,
She entered Carmel.
On her last day at home in Breslau
She prayed with her mother in the synagogue.

*

Canonization is a process.
Rome discerned
In the stench of burning Jewish flesh
The odour of sanctity.

High time,
However questionable the miracle,
To proclaim a Jewish saint.
Atonement
For the centuries of slaughter in the name of Christ,
The blood libel,
The compliance of the German bishops,
The silence of the popes.

Confessor and martyr.
There were no martyrs in the Shoah.
None died for their beliefs.

Bloodletting,
To purify the race.
She was executed, like the others,
Sister, brother, niece,
As just another Jew.

*

The chosen stumble out at Auschwitz.
They obey
The order to undress, and take their towels
Into the white cottage.

Stripped to their essential selves,
They stand beneath the showerheads
And breathe death.

Smoke rises from the crematorium.
Burnt offerings.
Reduction
To dust and ashes.

*

She died as Edith Stein.
She lived as Sister Benedicta of the Cross.

Drawn into God through the sign of contradiction,
A stumbling block to her people,
She inhabited mystery, an invisible world
Of grace and vicarious atonement,
Learning by a life of menial tasks and prayer
How to live at the Lord's hand.

In silent hours before the tabernacle,
Conversation,
More intimate than marriage.

The year she entered Carmel,
I talked, she said, with the Saviour,
And told him that I knew his cross
Was being laid on the Jewish people,
And I offered to take it up
In the name of all.

In spare hours
She completed a philosophical treatise,
Composed poems and meditations,
Corresponded with family and friends,
Attempted no conversions.

Waiting, on the Feast of the Holy Cross,
To renew her vows,
The day before her mother's agonizing death,
I felt, she wrote, her presence.

After Kristallnacht, and the transfer she requested
From Germany to Holland,
She offered herself to the heart of Jesus,
A sacrifice of propitiation,
For true peace.

In what was, she said, the twelfth hour,
She studied the Science of the Cross.

*

Holiness is a life.
Out of history, beyond phenomena,
Atonement.

The mystery of redemption lies in remembrance.

She is at one with her people,
With the Jew on the cross,
With the truth of God.

IV. A MATTER OF TIME

for G, 60 years on

AT SEVENTY

The face that greets him in this morning's mirror
Is smiling wryly, wiser than himself.
The promised age, it whispers. Three score and ten.
You enter now the country of the old.

Today's a borderline. Look backward then,
But not to linger. When were you ever
Happier than now? Look only long enough
To realize you've had a lucky life.

Look ahead, remembering to trust in God,
And take short views. Consider coming days,
However few or many, days of grace,
Knowing that's what all days have always been.

Looking outward's best. A comfortable home,
A decent income in retirement,
A tolerant wife, grown children still on speaking terms,
Grandchildren fond in spite of age and distance.

As for looking inward, don't. Today
Is not the time. When will it ever be?
Spend a happy birthday, basking in
Your family and friends' congratulations:

The inward look's still more than you can bear.

A BOX OF BONSAI

For our small flat, small trees. This Christmas,
I give you not the trees

But possibilities. The seeds require
Patience and care. A month or more

They must linger underneath the lid,
Winter in the fridge, before

The warm spring darkness of the cupboard
And a steady soak. A further month

Until the seedlings' leaves have opened, ready
For daylight, burgeoning, transplanting,

And transformation. Come this April,
They will take shape beneath your loving hands

And flourish. Like our children. Like
The greenwood of our marriage.

EASTER VIGIL

29 March 1997

1. Above, a clear night sky, the comet's glow.
   Below, upon the lawn beside the church,
   We gather for the lighting and the blessing.

   Make this new fire holy, and inflame us with new hope.

   This is the passover of the Lord. This
   Is the passover of the comet.

2. Out of deep space, deep time,
   Bright head and tail, a blazing apparition,
   It comes again on its determined round.

   Mock resurrection, godlike visitation,
   It casts a cold light on our ritual.

   It has overseen beginnings.

   It will overlook our end.

3. The celebrant uplifts the Paschal Candle.
   He carves a cross into the wax,
   Alpha above, Omega below,
   1 • 9 • 9 • 7 between the arms.

   Christ yesterday and today.
   The beginning and the end. All time
   Belongs to him, and all the ages.

   Another cross, five grains of incense
   Inserted for his wounds. And then
   The lighting of the Candle from new fire.

May the light of Christ, rising in glory,
Dispel the darkness of our hearts and minds.

Lumen Christi. Our candles lit, we follow
Into the church's darkened sanctum.
Lumen Christi. Deo Gratias.

4. More than a hundred million miles beyond
This speck on which we celebrate
His passing through the void from death to life,

A relic of our solar system's
Primordial matter, orbiting
Through four millennia, eroding
Through ten million years,

Particles of dust, hot molecules of gas,
Streaming in the solar wind.

Facts are not enough. It cannot be to us
Merely an enormous ball of rock and ice.

5. Out of deep time, the human brain evolved,
A hundred billion nerve-cells, more
Than the stars that punctuate the evening sky,

Programmed to invent a self, a soul,
To question, doubt, deny, believe,
Living in divided and distinguished worlds,

To calculate, beyond imagining,
Deep space, deep time, invest
A comet's fly-by with portentousness,

Elucidate its motions as a symbol
Of meaningless order, the indifference of nature, sign
Of our insignificance,

Divine its mystery as handiwork,
A signature, a curse, a blessing.

6. *Lumen Christi.* The Paschal Candle
Bravely burns before the altar.

Exsultet. The candles in our hands illuminate
Our faces. We raise our hearts and voices to the Lord
In thanks and praise.

Out of deep godhead into space and time
He came, to share our manhood, suffer
Distinction and disjunction,

To focus ordinary light, and shine upon us
The coherent light of God.

AT THE CREMATORIUM

It is all very tidy. In the trim brick building,
After prayers and hymns,
A button is discreetly pressed, the conveyor belt
Hums softly, and the coffin slowly
Proceeds beyond the curtain.

It lacks fire. Offstage, the sanitized reduction
Of flesh to ashes.
Our pagan forebears did it better. A cleansing blaze,
A visible flame to signify
The spirit's aspiration.

Inhumation's best. Daylight, an open grave.
Our tendering the body
To fresh-turned earth acknowledges its origin,
Attests our hope of resurrection,
And celebrates creation.

KITE

Bright tissue stretched on balsa bones,
Of itself this flimsy artifice
Can get up to nothing.

A breath, and it is groundless,
Becomes what it was meant to be,
A songless mockery of bird,

An incarnation of the air.
Taut string controls it. It tugs
Against the string. It wills

Autonomy. Freedom
To find its own direction,
Its flight path to destruction.

ICE SCULPTURE

Crystalline, not crystal: no hardened
        Soil but solid water;
    Fresh hewn, translucent goddess,
    Nude girl, glossed by winter sun.

Hand-crafted, like home-made quilts and pastries,
        And perfectly useless:
    Evanescent artifice,
    A making for the moment.

It will not gather dust, a statue stored
        In memory's museum.
    The sculptor takes a photo,
    Chronicles impermanence.

It blazes at day's end. Clarifies tomorrow's
        Sunstruck liquefaction,
    Assumption to earth and air,
    Elemental consummation.

IN THIN AIR

Standstill. A cloudscape stage set
Glides slowly past our cloister.

Abstracted from routine, sustained within
A frail cell by recycled breath,

Transcendent in a transient iceland,
We squander time. We drowse;

We scan a magazine, half gaze
At fabricated figures on a screen,

As soft floes unattended cross
The corners of our eyes. Here

If anywhere, still point, should be
A place for prayer. But no:

Passive, suspended in
This nowhere, we await release

From our cocoon—the tilt of wing,
The vibrant breakthrough that will bring us

Down to earth, the solid world
In sight again, and we,

Our seatbelts fastened, free to pray
For a smooth landing, and a glad

Re-entry to the life of keeping
One's feet upon the ground.

TWO AMERICAN TOWNS

1. *Ogunquit, Maine*

Is there a town here, somewhere,
A proper town, where people know their neighbours
And greet them every day?

Somewhere beyond this traffic-glutted
Tapeworm of a main street, twisting through the guts of the shore,
With hotels, hotels, hotels,

Restaurants, and shops to lure the tourists
Here for the beach, the deep-sea fishing, the whale-watch,
Or the colour of the leaves come Fall.

Strolling Shore Road, or riding on the trolley,
You pass the Baptist Church, the Methodist, the Public Library,
A small cemetery, not all its gravestones old,

A side road here and there marked PRIVATE.
There must be a town here somewhere,
A New England Brigadoon, apparent

After Columbus Day, when the hotels,
The shops and restaurants shut down, and the trolley
Stops running till mid-May. Or do the natives,

Once foliage no longer lights the trees,
Migrate, leaving this a ghost town,
To see the winter out in Florida?

2. *Garfield, New Jersey*

Just one more town you pass along the highway
In driving to or from New York. The name recalls
An undistinguished President, a cartoon cat.

No tourist centre here, no local postcards,
Not even of the tavern boasting that it serves
Warm Beer & Lousy Food.

A place you'd never think to visit
Unless you've family here. Just another
American town, founded as a haven

For Poles, Italians, Germans, Slovaks,
Worshipping in separate churches, their common ground
The Town Hall and the High School.

There's a Polish Foods section in the A & P,
But the liturgy at Holy Trinity Lutheran
Isn't Slovak any more. The lines between

Ethnic patches are becoming blurred,
Like the town's borders. A melting pot, a place
For living in, neat lawns and well-kept houses,

Friendly neighbours. Our souvenirs,
Photos of Robert and Meg, Phoebe and Marvin,
For the family album.

LEVITIES

1. A BROOD OF BRONTËS

Now the stormy day is over
And the stormy night comes down,
Anne is scribbling in the study,
Bran is boozing in the town,

Charlotte's dreaming of her Belgian,
Emily's dreaming Lord knows what,
Papa Patrick snores a sermon,
Auntie pisses in the pot.

As the wind and hail continue
Through another Yorkshire dawn,
Sisters, brother, aunt, and father
Curse the day that they were born.

2. FOLLY

At most it offers shelter from the rain. Otherwise,
Useless as a Wodehouse novel, this bridge at the far
          End of the meadow joins

Nothing to nowhere. Had you a ladder you could mount
From one side or the other, stroll to the middle, lean upon
          Its florid balustrade to view

  Nothing worth the effort. Underneath it nothing
  But grass has ever flowed. It occupies its air
  Serenely, like its lichens, for two centuries

  Taking the eye to tickle or offend with pure
  Frivolity. Wodehouse in his nineties still
  Delighted in Lord Emsworth and his Empress.

3. GERIATRIC NOTE

Old age means taking
Inordinate interest in
The erratic behaviour
Of one's lower intestine.

4. MARKET REPORT

Yesterday's Arts Council Index
Announced a further fall in poetry shares
Due to overproduction, and the recent drop

In interest rates. Armitage
Has declined another dozen points; Motion
Is holding steady. There's been a slight rise

In Anglo-Welsh Ltd, thanks to the Assembly,
But rumours persist that Post-Modernists Inc
Is on the brink of bankruptcy.

The quarterly critical survey
Forecasts a squeeze on imaginative liquidity
With deflationary effect. Analysts advise

Cutting back on stanzas, tightening
Controls on free verse, and diversifying
Into fiction and biography.

The Confederation of British Poetry
Has blamed the downturn on the internet,
And called for government intervention.

5. OLD WOMEN AND STICKS

In Welsh it rains, not cats and dogs,
But *hen wragedd a ffyn*.
And today, as we lounged in the local pub,
They hobbled in,

A coven of octogenarians
Bent on making merry,
Sat themselves down with a clatter of canes
And ordered sherry.

Dressed in their Sunday best, wrinkled faces
Powdered and rouged, white hair
Freshly permed, they sipped and gossiped
Almost an hour there

While it poured outside. Then with a flurry,
As the raindrops abated,
They tottered to the door, and in sudden sunshine
Evaporated.

6. PINGO

for Gillian Clarke and David Thomas, after dipping into the OED

There is no word in English for the dent
In upper lips the Welsh call *swch*. It's strange
So flexible a tongue should not invent
Or steal a term, and so extend its range.

But there's still hope, however late the date.
"We need no name for rounded nunataks,"
L. Koch declared in 1928—
And yet the urge to name could not relax.

What can one call a mound that snow and ice
In thawing have left hollow at the crest,
If asked to be both graphic and precise?

A "dipple"? No. Or, possibly, a "ringo"?
Geologists pooh-poohed: "The Eskimos know best",
And promptly added "pingo" to our lingo.

BREVITIES

ABSENT FRIEND
i. m. Ron MacGregor

Few meetings, frequent letters—latterly
Battlefield dispatches,
And now, a silence. Friendship
Lasts, however great the distance.

***

11 SEPTEMBER 2001

Never mind the voices urging
Retaliation and revenge,
Or that hours after the towers fell
And the great wave of dust engulfed the fugitives
Debris was for sale on the internet
As souvenirs:

Two Welsh neighbours, that Tuesday evening,
Both over ninety,
Voices shaking, tears on their cheeks,
Came to our door expressing their grief
To the only Americans they know:

There is a light that shines in darkness
And the darkness will not overcome it.

***

EPITAPH FOR A GARDENER
i. m. Ann Greig

Plants cannot mourn, but her flowers, missing
The green of her fingers,
Are withering, and the ground
That she tended has lost heart.

***

GRAVESTONES

St Michael's, Aberystwyth

They knew their place. A seaside churchyard's testament,
Through these mute tongues the earthfast generations
Informed our transient lives.

The dead have been transplanted. Where the churchyard was,
A playground and a garden. The gravestones line
The walks and garden walls,

Legends of fact and faith and love. Their silent voices
Still mingle with the shrill cries of the children
And the scent of roses.

***

GRENVILLE ROCKS

Seventy years ago, in Central Park,
We'd climb the rocks. Time has shrunk
The cliff that towered like an Everest,
Although I could not climb it now.

The present was our only tense. Deaf
To the indifferent schist beneath
The worn soles of our sneakers, whispering
Of the mountain it had been,

And of a sea that held within its womb
The possibility of us.

***

HAPPENSTANCE

Now
explodes, pure
moment, timeless
disruption of space and time,
as a cliffside rock
shatters the lake's pacific
surface:

Then
before and after
resume, cause and effect
repair the rent in time,
as the wound in the water
closes. The wound in the heart
remains.

***

HARBINGERS

Overcast again. But still,
Against the February morning cold,

These crocuses unfurl. Yellow, lavender,
They open tiny beaks to prophesy

Rebirth. And from the sycamore's
Bare bones a blackbird's golden bill

Carols a glad Amen.

***

A HIVE OF BEES

Donated at Christmas 2001 to a charity dedicated to alleviating hunger and poverty through gifts of income-producing farm animals.

Let them tend the swarm with reverence.
Let them hear in its hum a sacred chorus,

Recalling that by parthenogenesis
These creatures once were thought to be conceived.

Sweetness and light. Virgin and Child.
Let beeswax candles blaze for midnight mass

And bread and honey be the morning meal.
Let them tell the bees, as once, of births and deaths,

And let the hive be simulacrum of a tomb
From which they rise at dawn and soar into the sunlight.

***

IN A COUNTRY CHURCHYARD

Upon these stones, painstakingly inscribed
To honour and retain a loved one's memory,
Indecipherable traces
Of words and dates remain.
Wind and rain with their indifferent tears
Have scrawled a plain *memento mori.*

***

LOVEBIRDS

They should be doves, this pair of gulls
That every evening perches
On the roof-ridge opposite our window.

Like us, a contented couple, pleased
To be in one another's company,
In the light of the setting sun.

***

MARGINAL

As the tide withdraws
In traceries of lace,
The strand sprouts eyes and claws
And mouths that graze the furrows,
Frenetic race,
Until the water turns, extends
A lapping tongue, and finds
Only the mud that snugly roofs their burrows.

***

POLYP

Precious flesh, you're full of surprises.
This peduncular tumour now,
Mushroom in my intestine,
I'm told it's benign, but nonetheless
Something to keep one's eye on.

You're mine, I insist, not me, although
What would I be without you?
You'll win, I'm aware, in the end,
If it's winning to eliminate
The two of us together. Unless

What's promised in the creed proves true,
And we rise, eternally one being,
Me and you.

***

SHOAH

Enlightenment
Shines through a yellowing lampshade made
Of Jewish skin.

***

SIMULACRUM

The sundried husk of a bee
On the back wall of the house,
Paper-thin, perfectly intact,

Quivers with every breath of breeze,
Clings to the rough red brick
As if it were a blossom.

***

SOUVENIR

for Mary MacGregor, Penhill Lodge, Myddfai

This keepsake of our visit
(A day when breeze-blown drizzle
Asperged tourist and pilgrim)

To God's pebble, insular icon,
Tossed in the sea, its bedrock
Saint's dove-cote and his pillow,

The small stone from Iona
On your window sill today,
Glacier-scarred gneiss, coarse schist,

Under the sun's inspiration
Glows, incarnate colours
Radiant, like the ripples
Of Love's grace through space and time.

***

VOCATION

i. m. Sister Judith Savard, RSHM

A sacred game, your play
With line and colour,

Celebration
Of incarnation,

Illumination
Of our here-and-now:

Thrice called, thrice blest,
As artist, teacher, nun,

Your single service of the Light.

***

WONDERLAND

Today he'd be arrested,
A cleric who liked little girls,
Told them fantastic stories,
And photographed them nude.

Who'd believe that he beheld,
Gazing at unfledged bodies,
Unbudded breasts, bare vulva,
Images of innocence?

A GREGYNOG TRIPTYCH

1. RETREAT

Across a border, out of ordinary time,
We attend the talks and readings, dine and stroll
The grounds of the estate. The great house

Is not as ancient as it looks,
All but one room Victorian artifact.
We spend the weekend lulled within its fiction,

Play at a way of life to which we dare not wish
To become accustomed. In bygone times
Our fathers would have sawn its timbers,

Hammered in its nails, our mothers
Baked its bread and swept its floors.
Beyond its doors, above a dip's trim grass,

A concrete bridge, its balustrades
Inhabited by statues whose worn stone
Is decorously overgrown with moss,

And paths that wind us through dark woods.
These trees last century closed off
The miner's cough. Gardens and lawns

Were watered by his sweat. His bones
Sustained the manor walls. And yet,
It is, with all its ghosts, a gracious place,

A sanctum for the would-be civilized,
A refuge that refreshes, and returns us
Across the border to our daily lives.

2. THIS HAND

This hand arrests you
at the crossroads

This hand is larger
than your own

It has never known
a wrist, a body

This hand stands upright
on the grass

It is unshaken
by any weather

Its cracks retain
the stain of time

This hand reflects
no mirror image

It is a left hand
sinister

This hand is stone-faced
open-handed

This hand gives nothing
This hand asks nothing

It holds no promise
of curse or blessing

Turn back, or walk
into the woods

This hand will offer
no direction

3. THE WILD GEESE AT GREGYNOG

To the pond, we say, giving to our walk
Not a destination but a terminus.
A mid-March afternoon, chill breeze,
Weak sunshine. Stark boughs and twigs
Seem dormant still, although in listless grass
Bright clumps of crocuses proclaim the spring.
A blackbird whistles his agreement. Files
Of daffodils stay huddled in their sheaths.

The pond is dull, its darkling surface
Unruffled by the reeds within the shallows
And ripples here and there where unseen fish
Catch bugs too small for sight. Dull, dull.
The only thing that could produce a stir
Is jumping in. Then suddenly

Two geese are gliding, side by side,
Out into the middle. Their easy progress
Leaves the pond untroubled,
But here is life in motion. No thrum of wings,
No soaring off as an epiphany:
Ignoring us, they linger at the centre,
Then circle back to what we now can see
Is a small island near the other side.

They vanish in the bushes, and we turn
Back to the road. The pond has been
A sort of destination after all.

VORTEX

1. Still in motion. Still upon the wall.
   Horses. Bison. Aurochs.

   The cave resounds to the soundless
   Pounding of their hooves. Deep within

   The darkness of deep time, they await
   An illuminating eye.

2. At the end of the tunnel, light.
   His sandstone tallow lamp
   Clarifies the blankness of the wall.

   Hand steady, fluent, a single stroke
   Defines the bounding line. This is not
   A horse, a bull, a bison.

   It is too small. You cannot walk around it.
   No grass. No trees. No river.
   It lives on rock. It floats, a figure

   Discovered in the wall, projected
   From the cave behind his eyes.

3. His images, millennia away, must bear
   The glare of our torches. No spirits live for us

   Incarnate in these shapes, shadows
   Of a world beyond the wall.

   Horses. Bison. Aurochs. They enter
   The cave behind our eyes.

   It remains a sanctum. We contemplate
   His handiwork, and learn with him

   What it is to be human.

VULTURE DREAMING

We have no beauty in your eyes, save when
We soar and glide.
Bare-faced scavengers, we squabble over carrion,
Up to our naked necks in blood,

Scoff, and leave to falcon, hawk, and eagle
The thrill of pursuit,
The targeting of prey, the stoop, the kill.
What matters to us is meat.

We have our softer moments. These billhooks tender
Our single hatchling
Choice strips of rotting flesh. In Ancient Egypt
We signified maternal love.

We have our function. If we live on other
Creatures' leavings,
We're purgatory birds. Except for us
The land would stink of putrefaction.

We put you in your place. Part of the food-chain.
An item on the menu.
Harbingers not of death but of death's aftermath,
We show you what you're made of.

PENGUIN DREAMING

Not like emperors. Like monks
We shuffle in a solemn
Procession over ice,
Though, unlike monks
Or emperors, we sometimes
Slide across a patch upon
Our bellies.

Antarctica's ascetics,
Involuntary votaries,
Programmed to home in,
Through sleet and April darkness,
On stark ancestral acres,
Our breeding ground within the continent's
Barren heart.
Pure as the driven snow the drive
Impelling us to
A frigid courtship,
A cold conjunction,
A nestless parenting.

We stand toe to toe. She transfers
Our single egg, I tuck it
Beneath my stomach fold.
She joins the mothers' march,
The trek for miles of frozen track
To open water. I am welcomed
To the fellowship of fathers.

DRAGONFLY DREAMING

As I was, you'd not have known me.
Masked and armoured, underwater monster
With enormous eyes,

I'd lurk in silt and reeds. Jet-propelled,
I'd scud to clench and masticate small fry
Between my pincers.

Year on year, I'd moult to magnify
Myself, till high and dry upon a rock,
Metamorphosis.

Shrug by shrug, I flex soft flesh to shuck
My carapace. I pump to swell my flaccid
Crumpled wings,

And snap them open, spread them wide
For good. I harden into rainbow. Air
Is now my element.

I patrol my patch of water, hover,
Flash forward, backward, zig-zag, copter
Straight up and down.

I plait six legs to fabricate a net
For wasps and flies. Time was, before the birds,
The air was mine,

My giant shadow menaced swamp and stream.
Diminished, I survive millennia,
A hunter still.

SLOTH DREAMING

Awake
a mere
five hours of the twenty-four,
I take,
content,
my time.

My limbs
climb
leisurely through minutes,
savouring
the moments,

until, through leaves and fruit,
I hook, and sway,
downside up,
my slowly
munching way.

At ease,
I sprawl
along a comfy branch.
I sense the tree's
breathing. I breathe
its breath.

Asleep
again,
I become a hairy
hourglass.
I show,
in sun and rain,
how pleasant it can be to simply pass
one's time.

HARE DREAMING

Before man came, I was here,
With mammoth and woolly rhino:
The wood-cat, broom-cat, gorse-cat,
The stag with the leathern horns.

No burrow for me. I lurk
Low in a form till twilight;
Fiddle-footed dew-dinger,
I graze night mazes through grass.
Mad my mating dance come March;
I can conceive while pregnant.
Pursued, wide-eyed side-starer,
Wind-swift, I shift, tack, veer.
Long-legged, sturdy-loined, large-hearted,
I'm strong meat for a stew-pot.

Until Christ's coming I served
Eostre, hare-brained earth-goddess.
I frisk through field and hedgerow
To kindle the spring's fresh fires;
I am the last sheaf of grain
Cut by the circling reapers.
My shadow is on the moon's
Birth, death, and resurrection.
Though witches assume my shape,
Loper up hill, wall-leaper,
When coursed by hounds my haven
Is beneath Melangell's hem.

A PRAYER FOR WALES

A translation of 'Gweddi dros Gymru', Lewis Valentine's hymn, to the tune of Sibelius' 'Finlandia'.

We raise our cry, Oh Father, for our land,
This comely vineyard given us to tend;
May your strong hand still keep it firm in faith,
A nest to nurture holiness and truth;
For your Son's sake, who paid for it in blood,
Create a Wales in your own likeness, Lord.

Oh let there come a day when God's fresh breeze
May breathe once more across our withered fields,
And the parched soil, by heaven's showers graced,
May be a fruitful garden dear to Christ,
And our old language, rising sweet and loud,
May praise with youthful joy the Lamb of God.

DANDELION

for Bobi Jones

To Welsh from French from Latin,
Dant y llew, the lion's tooth,
Because of its jagged leaves.
But in English it's become
A toothless lion. A dandy,
Bright gold buttons adorning
Wasteland waistcoats, detested
Intruder on tidy lawns.

Composite, weedy perennial,
It has its uses. Wine
Is distilled from the radiant petals;
Fresh-picked, the bitter young leaves
May be eaten in salads.
A strong diuretic. French
Now mocks it as *pissenlit.*

A flowerhead of flowers,
It will fade into its ghost.
Upon the naked hollow stalk,
Frail globe of, it awaits,
Tufted seeds, a whim of wind
To sail the air, and scatter
Largesse to impoverished ground.

TWICE BORN

for Catherine Jing, born in China 11 August 2000, adopted one year later and brought to the U. S. by our daughter Meg and her husband Steve

Your first birth was in August,
And in August, oceans away,
Second birth, as our twelfth grandchild.

August's the time of ripening,
Autumn's dawn, when half-grown lambs
Dot the green of Welsh hillsides.
And twelve's a hallowed number,
Twelve months in the turning year,
Twelve signs of the zodiac,
Twelve days of Christmas, twelve
Gates to the Holy City,
Twelve fruits on the Tree of Life:
It signifies fulfillment,
A cycle, a perfect round.

Now you begin to define
Yourself in terms of others,
Emily's sister, Meg and Steve's daughter,
Cousin and niece to a crowd
Of uncles, aunts, and cousins,
Dear grand-daughter to Cathy,
And dear grand-daughter to us:
One among many, but always
Your singular self where love's
Mystery's not divided,
Whole for one, as whole for all.

Known to each other only
In our smiling photographs,

Youngest and oldest, the bond
Of belonging knows no distance:
Welcome to the sacred circle,
A womb, a cradle, a home,
The sanctum of a family.

PISCES

for Evan Robert Clancy, born 8 March 2003, in Hawthorne, New Jersey

Our sycamore's in bud. A blackbird
Bobs and warbles on the tender twigs,

And finches flitter to their nest above
Our window. Birth-time, here as there.

Welcome. An ocean and three quarters
Of a century apart, we share

Birthday and birth-sign. Two fish,
Swimming in opposite directions,

You upstream, I down. You've slipped
Fresh from your cloistral pond to navigate

Our tidal river. Rejoice
In the christening current, frisk

Cheerful through clear brisk rapids, hang
Tranquil within the flow.

Fluent words, love's distant greeting,
Be this a keepsake till the great deep beckons,

And ICHTHUS bless our passage, child,
You upstream, and me down.

SPECIAL DELIVERY

for Maude Hannah Scott Clancy, born 8 April 2005,
two months prematurely, in Glasgow

So here you are, wee girl, a good deal
Earlier than expected, featherweight
Kickboxing from your cosy cloister, bursting
The nurturing bubble betimes, impatiently
Precipitating advent.

A welcome outcome. We'll give you, tiny
April bud, the best world that we're able,
Whose abrupt entry
Now brings to us, in your blest mite of flesh,
The joy of spring.

HOSPITAL VISIT

I miss you daily, though I see you
Every day. Togetherness
Is tongue-tied here. An in-between space,
A nowhere like an airport waiting-room,
Place of tense silences and awkward talk.

Soon, please, soon, we'll take once more
An ordinary walk in town.
We'll stroll from bank to bookshop, stop
For tea in a café. We'll resume
The easy conversation of our marriage,

And the comfortable silence of our living room

GALLSTONES

No pearls, dear, from your oyster. Concretions
Of cholesterol and pigment, jagged
Peach pits dredged from your interior,
They float now in a jar beside the tussy-mussy
On your bedside table,

Sometime parts of you, unwelcome
Outcomes of loved flesh I cannot love.
Keep them anyway. Not, as one nurse proposed,
Made into a bracelet or earrings,
Not, please, for display

Upon our mantel. Tuck them away
Within a bedroom drawer, something
To happen on from time to time,
In sunshine days a souvenir of pain,
A *memento mori.*

UMBRELLA

Odd valentine, perhaps, this curious
Contraption. Thin fabric
Taut on a frame of jointed ribs that slide
Up and down a rod.

Gaudy its canopy with bright-faced flowers.
Elsewhere, this
Beneath blue skies might serve you doubly as
A parasol.

But here in Wales, the seldom sunshine is
For basking in,
Not shutting out. There's shade enough already
At any season.

Drizzle or downpour, may this love-gift keep
Head dry, heart cheerful:
Unfurl its jaunty blossoms, defy boldly
The darkest sky.

AFTER SEVENTY

Another neighbour dead. The wife this time.
Did they, like us, wonder as they grew older
Which would be first?

Not that we speak of it. It has become for me
A nightly thought, a subtext to my prayer
For a good death.

I would like some night (but not too soon)
To go to bed, confess, thank God for you,
And not wake up.

A selfish thought, perhaps, leaving you to cope
With being half a couple. You would do it, though,
Better than I.

Meanwhile we rehearse. I learn to do
The laundry. You have yet to master tax forms
And the VTR.

A blessing, nonetheless, this living in the shadow
Of future separation. Time together is no longer
Taken for granted,

The waking side-by-side's a grace each morning,
And there's a special sweetness in our kiss
Before we sleep.

NOTES & ACKNOWLEDGEMENTS

Mission. The chain of Franciscan missions founded between 1769 and 1823 along 'the king's highway', *el camino real*, was created for secular as well as religious reasons. 'The church was responsible for the religious conversion of the people and the Spanish government was responsible for acquiring more land for the monarch' (Barbara Shangle, *California Missions*). Barracks for soldiers were therefore part of the complex of buildings, along with the monastery, workshops, granary, and church. The founder of this northernmost and last-constructed mission in Sonoma, Fr José Altimira, controlled the local Indians with flogging and imprisonment, and was transferred after a group of them attacked the mission. His successor, Fr Buenaventura Fortuni, was as good as his name, securing almost a thousand converts who farmed extensively and productively. As Shangle rather tactfully puts it, 'entering a land that was unexplored and encountering inhabitants who spoke unknown languages, and who maintained different values and beliefs from those of the padres and soldiers, led to fear and apprehension for all groups involved.'

MUSEUM PIECES. While I do not think it essential for experiencing these poems, I note here with gratitude the places where some of the works can be seen. *Ball.* The Royal Museum of Scotland, Edinburgh. *The Butterfly Connection.* The Museum of Science, Houston, Texas. *Cezanne's Mountain.* In his later years, Paul Cezanne, who had always been uncomfortable with live models, used museum photographs of pictures and sculptures for his paintings of bathers. He did 30 oils and 45 water-clours of Mont Ste-Victoire, near his birthplace in Aix-en-Provence. Three years before his death in 1906, Cezanne wrote that 'I am stubbornly going on with my work, for I am beginning to see the Promised Land.' I am indebted to Hajo Duchting's *Cezanne*, Philip Callow's *Lost Earth: A Life of Cezanne*, and Robert Hughes' *The Shock of the New* for information, illustrations, and commentaries. *The Exhumation of the Mastodon.* The poem is based on a photograph of the painting and information about the painter in Robert Hughes' *American Visions*. *Field of Corn.* An artwork by Malcolm Conran to commemorate what once was farmland. *Funeral Socks.* Exhibition of Welsh Folk Crafts, Arts

Centre, Aberystwyth. *Harpist.* Metropolitan Museum of Art, New York City. *Jesse.* St Mary's Priory Church, Abergavenny. *Looking at Rembrandt.* For information and illustrations I am indebted to Simon Schama's *Rembrandt's Eyes. Looking for Vermeer.* For information and illustrations I am indebted to Anthony Bailey's *A View of Delft: Vermeer Then and Now. Madonna.* The poem is based on Mantegna's depiction of Mary in his painting The Dead Christ. *Misericords.* The Parish Church of Saint Laurence, Ludlow. *Relic.* St. Andrew's Cathedral, Scotland. *Screens.* The Kayama Matazo exhibit at The British Museum, London.

Bone Hunter. For information and some phrases, including a few from Cope's letters, I am indebted to Henry Fairfield Osborn's *Cope: Master Naturalist*, Edwin H. Colbert's *Men and Dinosaurs*, and Uri Lanham's *The Bone Hunters: The Heroic Age of Paleontology in the American West.* Professor O. C. Marsh of Yale University, with greater wealth and political influence, impeded Cope's researches, and their bitter rivalry led to mutual attacks in scientific journals and the public press. A fellow palaeontologist, Professor W. B. Scott, noted 'Marsh's egotism, his intense selfishness, and his unscrupulous duplicity', but added that he 'was a very able man and rendered immense service to American palaeontology'.

Portrait of a Priest. Composed for the celebration by St. Winefride's parish of the jubilee of Fr. John Fitzgerald's ordination. A notable Welsh-language poet, Fr. Fitzgerald was at the time Catholic chaplain for the University of Wales, Aberystwyth, where for many years he taught philosophy through the medium of Welsh. *corlannau:* sheepfolds.

Benedicta. For information and quotations I am indebted to the following: *Edith Stein, Life in a Jewish Family*, edited by L. Gelber and Romaens Leuwen, translated by Josephine Koeppel; *Edith Stein, Self-Portrait in Letters*, translated by Josephine Koeppel; James Carroll, 'The Saint and the Holocaust', *The New Yorker (June 7, 1999)*, pp. 52-57; Freda Mary Oben, *The Life and Thought of St. Edith Stein*; Maria Ruiz Scaperlanda, *Edith Stein: St. Teresa Benedicta*; Waltraud Herbstrith, *Edith Stein: A Biography*; John Sullivan ed., *Edith Stein: Essential Writings*; Marianne Sawicki, *Body, Text, and*

Science: The Literacy of Investigative Practices and the Phenomenology of Edith Stein; Patricia Hampl, 'A Book Sealed with Seven Seals: Edith Stein', *I Could Tell You Stories*; Guenter Lewy, *The Catholic Church and Nazi Germany*. The italicized quotation in the first section is adapted from the official report of the Netherlands Red Cross in 1958; in the second section is Jeremiah 29: 14; in the final section is from the Holocaust memorial in Jerusalem.
her sister: Edith's older sister Rosa was baptized three months after their mother's death in 1936 and became a Third Order Carmelite. She was with Edith in the convents at Cologne and Echt, and died with her in Auschwitz.
the Science of the Cross: Edith Stein's own term for knowledge that 'can only be gained when one comes to feel the cross radically', and the title of her final unfinished work, a study of the life, theology, and poetry of St. John of the Cross.

Easter Vigil. In 1997 the Hale-Bopp comet was visible in the early evening from the lawn of St. Winefride's church, Aberystwyth, during the ceremony of lighting the new fire.

Grenville Rocks. The geological term for the remains of a Precambrian mountain chain in the northeastern United States. For the information on which the poem is based I am indebted to Richard Fortey's *The Earth*.

A Gregynog Triptych. Plas Gregynog, a large estate in Powys dating from the fifteenth century, was purchased in 1918 by colliery owner Lord Davies of Llandinam, a noted philanthropist and ardent supporter of the League of Nations. His unmarried sisters Gwendoline and Margaret collected French Impressionist paintings, established a private press famous for the quality of its limited editions, and from 1920 to 1940 sponsored musical programmes by international performers and major festivals of music and poetry at the Hall. Margaret Davies donated the estate to the University of Wales in 1960, and it is regularly used for conferences and concerts. The outdoor sculpture of a giant hand is by Francis Hewlett.

Vortex. For information, illustrations, and interpretations, I am indebted to Denis Vialou's *Our Prehistoric Past: Art and Civilization* and David Lewis-Williams' *The Mind in the Cave: Consciousness and the Origins of Art*.

Dragonfly Dreaming. For images and information I am indebted to David Attenborough's book and television programme *Life in the Undergrowt*h.

Hare Dreaming. I am indebted to *The Leaping Hare* by George Ewart Evans and David Thomson for information and their transcription of a thirteenth-century English poem on the names given to the hare. Eostre was an Anglo-Saxon fertility goddess whose name was retained in the Christian feast of Easter. Melangell, the Welsh patron saint of all small creatures, was a sixth-century Irish princess who escaped the marriage her father had arranged for her by fleeing to Wales. She is said to have hidden a hare under her robes to save it from the hounds of the Prince of Powys, who because of her sanctity gave her the land around the present-day village of Pennant Melangell, where she founded a community of nuns and a twelfth-century church still stands.

"Fog in Applewood Lane", was a specially commended poem in the BBC Wildlife Poetry Competition 2000 and published on the website. "Bone Hunter" was a commended long poem in the Third Scintilla Open Poetry Competition and published in *Scintilla 6*. "Kite", "Nonagenarian", and "Relic", were published in Peter Read and Sally Roberts Jones' anthology *Over Milk Wood.* "This Hand" was published in Kathy Miles' anthology of photographs and poems, *The Third Day*, and "Funeral Socks" in the PHRAS anthology for 1996. Other poems first appeared in *Acumen*, *Cambria*, *The Interpreter's House*, *New Welsh Review*, *Planet*, *RPS 6*, *Roundyhous*e, *Scintilla*, *The Spectator*, and *Thumbscrew*.

Joseph P. Clancy was born in 1928 in New York City, where he lived until he retired in 1990 and settled in Wales. He holds his Ph.D. from Fordham University and is Marymount Manhattan College's Emeritus Professor of English Literature.

In addition to his poems, he has translated extensively from Welsh literature, and with his wife Gertrude co-authored a mystery novel, *Death Is A Pilgrim: A Canterbury Tale*, featuring Geoffrey Chaucer as detective. His recent books include *Other Words: Essays on Poetry and Translatio*n, and a large anthology of *Medieval Welsh Poems* in translation.

He is a Fellow of the English-Language Section of Yr Academi Gymreig (The Welsh Academy) and an Honorary Fellow of the University of Wales, Aberystwyth. He was awarded an honorary D. Litt. by the University of Wales for his work as poet and translator.